CLASSICAL THEMES
FOR VIOLIN DUET

Arranged by Michelle Hynson

ISBN 978-1-5400-9735-4

For all works contained herein:
Unauthorized copying, arranging, adapting, recording, internet posting, public performance,
or other distribution of the music in this publication is an infringement of copyright.
Infringers are liable under the law.

Visit Hal Leonard Online at
www.halleonard.com

Contact us:
Hal Leonard
7777 West Bluemound Road
Milwaukee, WI 53213
Email: info@halleonard.com

In Europe, contact:
Hal Leonard Europe Limited
42 Wigmore Street
Marylebone, London, W1U 2RN
Email: info@halleonardeurope.com

In Australia, contact:
Hal Leonard Australia Pty. Ltd.
4 Lentara Court
Cheltenham, Victoria, 3192 Australia
Email: info@halleonard.com.au

AIR
(Air on the G String)
from ORCHESTRAL SUITE NO. 3 IN D MAJOR, BWV 1068

By JOHANN SEBASTIAN BACH

VIOLIN

Andante

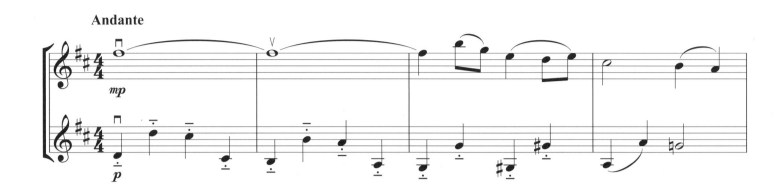

Copyright © 2021 by HAL LEONARD LLC
International Copyright Secured   All Rights Reserved

BY THE BEAUTIFUL BLUE DANUBE

VIOLIN

By JOHANN STRAUSS, JR.

Copyright © 2021 by HAL LEONARD LLC
International Copyright Secured   All Rights Reserved

+ = left-hand pizzicato

CANON IN D

VIOLIN

By JOHANN PACHELBEL

Copyright © 2021 by HAL LEONARD LLC
International Copyright Secured   All Rights Reserved

DANCE OF THE SUGAR PLUM FAIRY

from THE NUTCRACKER SUITE, OP. 71A

VIOLIN

By PYOTR IL'YICH TCHAIKOVSKY

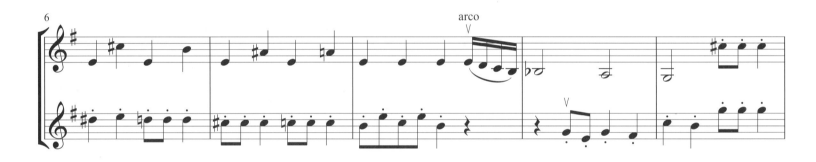

Copyright © 2021 by HAL LEONARD LLC
International Copyright Secured   All Rights Reserved

EIN MÄDCHEN ODER WEIBCHEN

from THE MAGIC FLUTE (DIE ZAUBERFLÖTE)

VIOLIN

By WOLFGANG AMADEUS MOZART

Copyright © 2021 by HAL LEONARD LLC
International Copyright Secured   All Rights Reserved

EINE KLEINE NACHTMUSIK
("Serenade")
First Movement Excerpt

VIOLIN

By WOLFGANG AMADEUS MOZART

Copyright © 2021 by HAL LEONARD LLC
International Copyright Secured   All Rights Reserved

FLOWER DUET
from LAKME

VIOLIN

By LEO DELIBES

Gently flowing

Copyright © 2021 by HAL LEONARD LLC
International Copyright Secured   All Rights Reserved

HORNPIPE
from WATER MUSIC

VIOLIN

By GEORGE FRIDERIC HANDEL

Copyright © 2021 by HAL LEONARD LLC
International Copyright Secured   All Rights Reserved

IN THE HALL OF THE MOUNTAIN KING

from PEER GYNT

VIOLIN

By EDVARD GRIEG

Copyright © 2021 by HAL LEONARD LLC
International Copyright Secured   All Rights Reserved

LA DONNA È MOBILE
from RIGOLETTO

VIOLIN

By GIUSEPPE VERDI

Allegretto

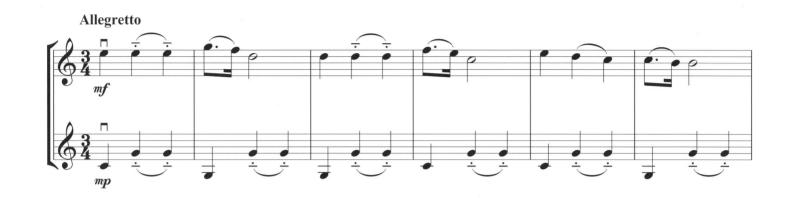

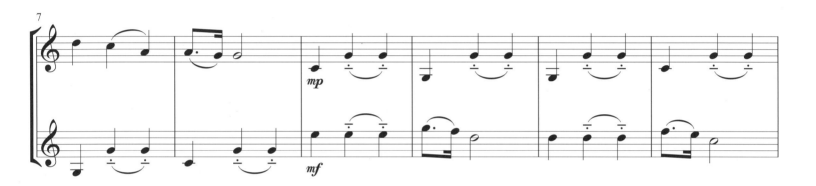

Copyright © 2021 by HAL LEONARD LLC
International Copyright Secured   All Rights Reserved

LARGO
from SYMPHONY No. 9 in E MINOR, Op. 95
("From the New World")

VIOLIN

By ANTONÍN DVOŘÁK

Copyright © 2021 by HAL LEONARD LLC
International Copyright Secured   All Rights Reserved

LIEBESTRAUM No. 3
(Dream of Love)

VIOLIN

By FRANZ LISZT

Copyright © 2021 by HAL LEONARD LLC
International Copyright Secured   All Rights Reserved

LULLABY

VIOLIN

By JOHANNES BRAHMS

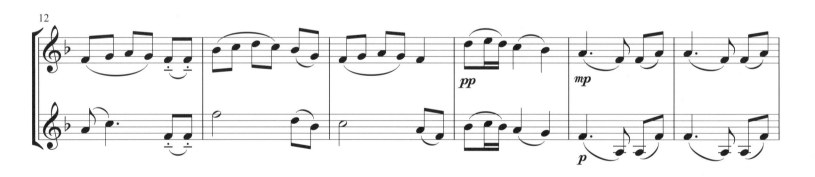

Copyright © 2021 by HAL LEONARD LLC
International Copyright Secured   All Rights Reserved

MORNING

from PEER GYNT

VIOLIN

By EDVARD GRIEG

Copyright © 2021 by HAL LEONARD LLC
International Copyright Secured   All Rights Reserved

NIGHT ON BALD MOUNTAIN

VIOLIN

By MODEST MUSSORGSKY

Copyright © 2021 by HAL LEONARD LLC
International Copyright Secured   All Rights Reserved

PAVANE DE LA BELLE AU BOIS DORMANT
(Sleeping Beauty Pavane)
from MOTHER GOOSE SUITE

VIOLIN

By MAURICE RAVEL

Copyright © 2021 by HAL LEONARD LLC
International Copyright Secured   All Rights Reserved

POLOVETSIAN DANCE THEME

VIOLIN

By ALEXANDER BORODIN

Copyright © 2021 by HAL LEONARD LLC
International Copyright Secured   All Rights Reserved

POMP AND CIRCUMSTANCE
March No. 1, Op. 39

VIOLIN

By EDWARD ELGAR

Copyright © 2021 by HAL LEONARD LLC
International Copyright Secured   All Rights Reserved

PROMENADE THEME

from PICTURES AT AN EXHIBITION

VIOLIN

By MODEST MUSSORGSKY

Moderately

Copyright © 2021 by HAL LEONARD LLC
International Copyright Secured   All Rights Reserved

RÊVERIE

VIOLIN

By CLAUDE DEBUSSY

Copyright © 2021 by HAL LEONARD LLC
International Copyright Secured   All Rights Reserved

RHAPSODY IN BLUE

VIOLIN

By GEORGE GERSHWIN

Copyright © 2021 by HAL LEONARD LLC
International Copyright Secured   All Rights Reserved

RIDE OF THE VALKYRIES
from DIE WALKÜRE

VIOLIN

By RICHARD WAGNER

Copyright © 2021 by HAL LEONARD LLC
International Copyright Secured   All Rights Reserved

SHEEP MAY SAFELY GRAZE

from CANTATA, BWV 208

VIOLIN

By JOHANN SEBASTIAN BACH

Copyright © 2021 by HAL LEONARD LLC
International Copyright Secured   All Rights Reserved

THE SLEEPING BEAUTY WALTZ

VIOLIN

By PYOTR IL'YICH TCHAIKOVSKY

Copyright © 2021 by HAL LEONARD LLC
International Copyright Secured   All Rights Reserved

SPRING
from THE FOUR SEASONS

VIOLIN

By ANTONIO VIVALDI

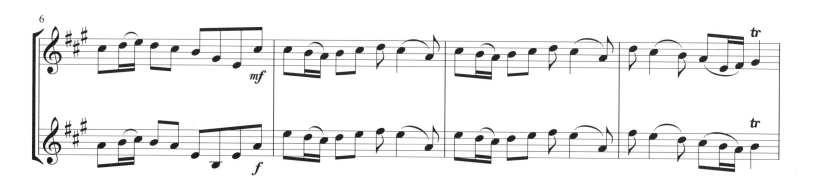

Copyright © 2021 by HAL LEONARD LLC
International Copyright Secured   All Rights Reserved

THE SWAN
(Le Cygne)
from CARNIVAL OF THE ANIMALS

VIOLIN

By CAMILLE SAINT-SAËNS

Copyright © 2021 by HAL LEONARD LLC
International Copyright Secured   All Rights Reserved

SYMPHONY No. 5 in C MINOR
(First Movement Excerpt)

VIOLIN

By LUDWIG VAN BEETHOVEN

Copyright © 2021 by HAL LEONARD LLC
International Copyright Secured   All Rights Reserved

TOREADOR SONG
from CARMEN

VIOLIN

By GEORGES BIZET

Copyright © 2021 by HAL LEONARD LLC
International Copyright Secured   All Rights Reserved

TRÄUMEREI
(Dreaming), Op. 15, No. 7
from SCENES FROM CHILDHOOD (KINDERSZENEN), OP. 15, NO. 7

VIOLIN

By ROBERT SCHUMANN

Copyright © 2021 by HAL LEONARD LLC
International Copyright Secured   All Rights Reserved

WILLIAM TELL OVERTURE

VIOLIN

By GIOACHINO ROSSINI

Copyright © 2021 by HAL LEONARD LLC
International Copyright Secured   All Rights Reserved

VIOLIN DUET
COLLECTIONS

These collections are designed for violinists familiar with first position and comfortable reading basic rhythms. Each two-page arrangement includes a violin 1 and violin 2 part, with each taking a turn at playing the melody for a fun and challenging ensemble experience.

ALL-TIME POPULAR SONGS FOR VIOLIN DUET

Billie Jean • Bridge over Troubled Water • Can You Feel the Love Tonight • Hallelujah • Imagine • Over the Rainbow • Unchained Melody • What a Wonderful World • With or Without You • Your Song and more.

00222449 . . . . $14.99

THE BEATLES FOR VIOLIN DUET

All My Loving • Blackbird • Eleanor Rigby • A Hard Day's Night • Hey Jude • Let It Be • Michelle • Ob-La-Di, Ob-La-Da • Something • When I'm Sixty-Four • Yesterday and more.

00218245 . . . . $12.99

POP HITS FOR VIOLIN DUET

All of Me • Hello • Just the Way You Are • Let It Go • Love Yourself • Ophelia • Riptide • Say Something • Shake It Off • Story of My Life • Take Me to Church • Thinking Out Loud • Wake Me Up! and more.

00217577 . . . . $14.99

DISNEY SONGS FOR VIOLIN DUET

Beauty and the Beast • Can You Feel the Love Tonight • Colors of the Wind • Do You Want to Build a Snowman? • Hakuna Matata • How Far I'll Go • I'm Wishing • Let It Go • Some Day My Prince Will Come • A Spoonful of Sugar • Under the Sea • When She Loved Me • A Whole New World and more.

00217578 . . . . $14.99

www.halleonard.com

Prices, contents, and availability subject to change without notice.